Fun and Simple State Crafts

Fun and Simple
Great Lakes
State Crafts

Michigan, Ohio, Indiana, Illinois, Wisconsin, and Minnesota

June Ponte

Enslow Elementary

an imprint of

Enslow Publishers, Inc.

40 Industrial Road
Box 398
Berkeley Heights, NJ 07922
USA

http://www.enslow.com

This book meets the National Council for the Social Studies standards.

Enslow Elementary, an imprint of Enslow Publishers, Inc.

Enslow Elementary® is a registered trademark of Enslow Publishers, Inc.

Library of Congress Cataloging-in-Publication Data

Ponte, June.
    Fun and simple Great Lakes state crafts : Michigan, Ohio, Indiana, Illinois, Wisconsin, and
        Minnesota / June Ponte.
           p. cm. — (Fun and simple state crafts)
    Summary: "Provides facts and craft ideas for each of the states that make up the Great Lakes
        region of the United States"—Provided by publisher.
    Includes bibliographical references and index.
    ISBN-13: 978-0-7660-2983-5
    1. Handicraft—Lake States—Juvenile literature. I. Title.
    TT23.3.P66 2009
    745.50977—dc22

                                2007051782

ISBN-10: 0-7660-2983-2

Printed in the United States of America

10 9 8 7 6 5 4 3 2 1

To Our Readers: We have done our best to make sure all Internet Addresses in this book were active and appropriate when we went to press. However, the author and the publisher have no control over and assume no liability for the material available on those Internet sites or on other Web sites they may link to. Any comments or suggestions can be sent by e-mail to comments@enslow.com or to the address on the back cover.

Every effort has been made to locate all copyright holders of material used in this book. If any errors or omissions have occurred, corrections will be made in future editions of this book.

♻ Enslow Publishers, Inc., is committed to printing our books on recycled paper. The paper in every book contains 10% to 30% post-consumer waste (PCW). The cover board on the outside of each book contains 100% PCW. Our goal is to do our part to help young people and the environment too!

Illustration Credits: Crafts prepared by June Ponte; Photography by Nicole diMella/Enslow Publishers, Inc.; © 1999 Artville, LLC., pp. 6–7; Corel Corporation, pp. 9 (deer), 21 (flower), 27 (flower), 33 (animal), 39 (bird); © 2007 Jupiterimages, all clipart and pp. 15 (all), 21 (birds), 27 (fish), 33 (bird), 39 (animal); © 2001 Robesus, Inc., all state flags; Shutterstock, p. 9 (bird).

Cover Illustration: Crafts prepared by June Ponte; Photography by Nicole diMella/Enslow Publishers, Inc.; © 1999 Artville, LLC., map; © Jupiterimages, state buttons.

CONTENTS

Welcome to the Great Lakes Region!

Michigan, Ohio, Indiana, Illinois, Wisconsin, and Minnesota are the six states in the Great Lakes region. This area is referred to as the Great Lakes region because these states border four of the five Great Lakes of the United States. The lakes are Lake Superior, Lake Michigan, Lake Huron, and Lake Erie.

The geography of the Great Lakes states is mainly flatlands, prairies, and river valleys.

Most people think of the automobile industry when they think of Michigan. This state is also known for its 3,300 miles of shoreline, its lakes, and its many forests. Lansing is the capital of Michigan, but Detroit is the largest city in the state.

Ohio is located between Lake Erie and the Ohio River. The state has rolling hills in the southern area. The land is more level in the north. Once covered by buckeye tree forests, Ohio is now an important industrial state.

Indiana has a combination of flatlands in the north and land that is mostly hilly in the south. There are more than five hundred lakes in Indiana. Hoosier National Forest covers 200,00 square miles in the hills of southern Indiana.

Illinois is mostly flat and is known as the "Prairie State." The Chicago River runs through Chicago, which is located on Lake Michigan's shore. The Central Plains, the Gulf Coastal Plain, and the Shawnee Hills are Illinois' three regions.

Wisconsin's twenty-two Apostle Islands are in Lake Superior, at the northern part of the state. Winters are very cold in Wisconsin, and people enjoy snowmobiling and other cold-weather outdoor activities. The state covers 65,500 square miles and shares a border with Lake Michigan, Lake Superior, Minnesota, Michigan, Illinois, and Iowa.

Minnesota is hot and humid in the summertime and is cold with lots of snowfall in the winter. There are thousands of lakes in the state, which were formed by glaciers long ago. The state has many plains. The northeastern area has rocky, ridged areas. In the southeastern section of the state, near the Mississippi River, the land is mainly flat.

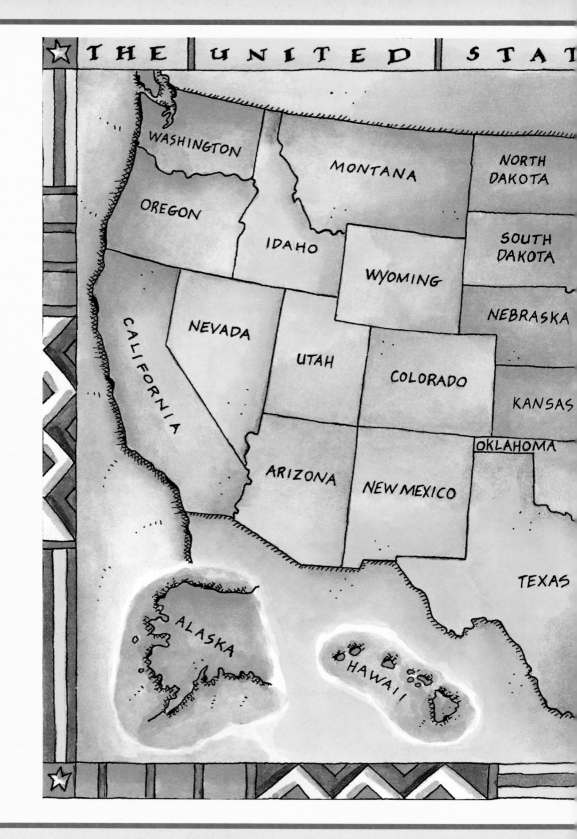

MINNESOTA

WISCONSIN

MICHIGAN

NEW.
HAMPSHIRE
VERMONT
MAINE

NEW YORK   MASSACHUSETTS

RHODE
ISLAND

CONNECTICUT

IOWA

ILLINOIS

INDIANA

OHIO

PENNSYLVANIA

NEW JERSEY

DELAWARE

MISSOURI

WEST
VIRGINIA

MARYLAND

WASHINGTON, D.C.

KENTUCKY

VIRGINIA

NORTH
CAROLINA

ARKANSAS

TENNESSEE

SOUTH
CAROLINA

MISSISSIPPI

ALABAMA

GEORGIA

N

LOUISIANA

FLORIDA

Great Lake States

MICHIGAN

Origin of name	*Michigan* comes from the Chippewa Indian word *Michigama* which means "great lake."
Flag	The Michigan state flag is blue. In the center of the flag is a coat of arms. The coat of arms shows a man standing on a peninsula, with the sun rising over the water. An elk and a moose are on either side of the coat of arms, and a bald eagle is on top of the crest. *E Pluribus Unum*, which means "Out of many, one," is written on a scroll above the eagle. *Tuebor*, meaning "I will defend," is written in the coat of arms at the top. In a scroll at the bottom of the crest are the words *Si quaeris peninsulam amoenam circumspice*, meaning "If you seek a pleasant peninsula, look around you."
Capital	Lansing
Nickname	The Wolverine State

Motto	*Si quaeris peninsulam amoenam circumspice* (This is a Latin phrase which means, "If you seek a pleasant peninsula, look around you.")
Size (in area)	11th largest
Animal	white-tailed deer
Bird	robin
Fish	brook trout
Flower	apple blossom
Tree	white pine
Industry	automobile manufacturing, agriculture, forestry, manufacturing, mining

CHERRY TABLE RUNNER

Michigan is the nation's top cherry-producing state. In Eau Claire, Michigan, a cherry pit spitting contest is held. The person who can spit a cherry pit the farthest wins. One person was able to spit a cherry pit more than ninety-three feet!

What you will need

* pencil
* paper or poster board
* scissors
* red felt
* masking tape
* white glue
* two pieces cream-colored felt
* green yarn
* small wooden beads

What you will do

1. Draw a cherry shape on paper or poster board. (See page 44 for the pattern.) Cut it out, and trace twelve cherries onto the red felt. Cut out the cherries (See A).

A)

B)

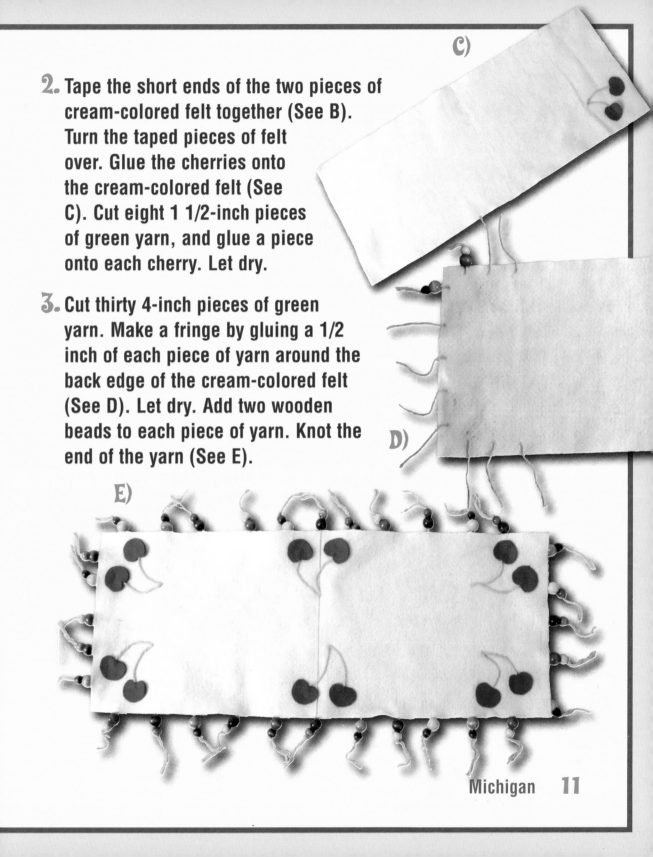

2. Tape the short ends of the two pieces of cream-colored felt together (See B). Turn the taped pieces of felt over. Glue the cherries onto the cream-colored felt (See C). Cut eight 1 1/2-inch pieces of green yarn, and glue a piece onto each cherry. Let dry.

3. Cut thirty 4-inch pieces of green yarn. Make a fringe by gluing a 1/2 inch of each piece of yarn around the back edge of the cream-colored felt (See D). Let dry. Add two wooden beads to each piece of yarn. Knot the end of the yarn (See E).

C)

D)

E)

FERRIS WHEEL

The Uniroyal Giant Tire has quite a history. This giant tire was made as a Ferris Wheel ride for the 1964–1965 World's Fair in New York.

When the World's Fair was over, the giant tire was brought to Detroit, Michigan. The Uniroyal Giant Tire is an important symbol of the tire and automobile industry in Detroit.

What you will need

* pencil
* plastic lid about 7 inches wide
* black construc-tion paper
* scissors
* silver glitter pen
* white glue
* hole punch
* black permanent marker
* large wooden beads
* small wooden beads (optional)
* 40 inches of yarn

What you will do

A)

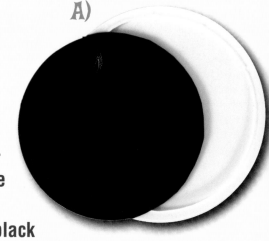

1. Cut a piece of black construction paper to fit inside the plastic container lid (See A).

2. Ask an adult to help you cut a 1/4-inch-long X in the center of the lid and in the center of the construction paper. Draw details with a silver glitter pen on the black

construction paper. Make it look like a tire. Glue the paper circle onto the lid. Let dry.

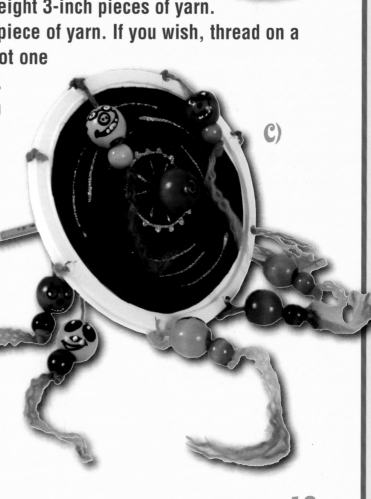

B)

3. Punch eight holes, evenly spaced, around the edge of the lid (See B). Set aside.

4. With a black marker, draw a face on each of eight wooden beads. Cut eight 3-inch pieces of yarn. Thread each bead onto a piece of yarn. If you wish, thread on a smaller wooden bead. Knot one end of each piece of yarn. Thread each piece of yarn with bead through a hole in the edge of the lid. Knot each piece of yarn (See C).

C)

5. Stick a pencil through the X cut in the center of the tire. Glue a bead to the top of the pencil. Let dry. Spin the pencil slowly, and watch the bead people go for a ride.

OHIO

Origin of name	The state of Ohio received its name from the Iroquois Indian word meaning "beautiful river."
Flag	The Ohio state flag is a swallowtail shape instead of a rectangle and has three red stripes and two white stripes. It has a triangle-shaped blue area decorated with seventeen white stars. Four of these stars are grouped separately. Thirteen of the stars represent the original thirteen colonies. Ohio became the seventeenth state to join the union. The four stars on the state flag added to the other stars represent Ohio's status as the seventeenth state to join the union. A red circle with a white border in the center of the blue triangle represents the *O* in Ohio.
Capital	Columbus

Nickname	The Buckeye State
Motto	"With God, all things are possible."
Size (in area)	34th largest
Animal	white-tailed deer
Bird	cardinal
Flower	scarlet carnation
Fossil	trilobite
Tree	buckeye
Industry	manufacturing steel, cars, airplanes; service industry; agriculture, including soybeans, dairy products, poultry, and eggs

15

RUBBER STAMP

In 1991, artists Claes Oldenburg and Coosje van Bruggen created a fifty-foot-tall rubber stamp sculpture. The artists put the word *FREE* on the stamp to represent our freedom as American citizens. This huge piece of art is displayed in Willard Park in Cleveland, Ohio.

What you will need

* pencil
* ruler
* cardboard
* scissors
* craft foam
* white glue
* ballpoint pen
* soda bottle cap
* poster paint
* foam paper plate
* index cards

What you will do

1. Draw a 5-inch by 2-inch rectangle on cardboard, and cut it out. Trace it onto craft foam. Cut out the craft foam, and glue onto the cardboard (See A). Let dry.

A)

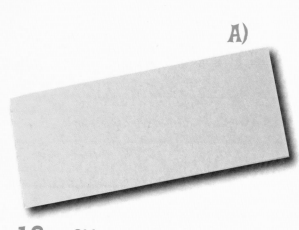

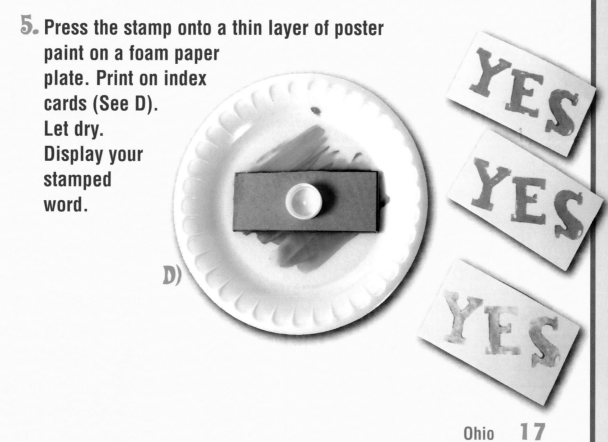

2. With a ballpoint pen, draw a word with five letters or less on another piece of craft foam. Cut out the letters. The letters should be about 1 1/2 inches tall (See B).

B)

C)

3. Glue the letters on the craft foam backward. The first letter of your word should be placed on the right side (See C).

4. Glue a soda bottle cap on the back of the cardboard. Let dry.

5. Press the stamp onto a thin layer of poster paint on a foam paper plate. Print on index cards (See D). Let dry. Display your stamped word.

D)

Hopewell Indian Clay Bird

What you will need

* ruler
* terra-cotta self-hardening clay
* toothpick
* poster paint
* paintbrush
* yarn

The Hopewell Indians lived from about 100 B.C. to A.D. 500. These people made unusual objects. The Hopewell Indians made pottery using clay found near their homes. They made many things from the clay, including pots, pipes, and animals. Many pieces of their pottery were found in the earth at Hopewell Culture National Historical Park in Ohio.

What you will do

1. Roll a piece of clay into a 1/2-inch-thick and 3-inch-wide by 5-inch-long flat piece.

2. Using a toothpick, draw the shape of a bird. (See page 46 for pattern.) Remove the extra clay from around the design. Near the top of the bird make a hole large enough for a piece of yarn to pass through. Using the toothpick, add details such as an eye, beak, feet, and feathers. Let dry.

3. Paint the bird with poster paint. Let dry. Thread a piece of yarn through the hole for hanging.

INDIANA

Origin of name	*Indiana* means "land of the Indians."
Flag	The Indiana state flag is blue with a gold-colored torch. Around the torch are thirteen stars in a circle, and inside that circle are five stars. The torch represents liberty and enlightenment. The circle of thirteen stars stands for the thirteen original American colonies. The next five states to join the Union are represented by the five stars inside the circle. Indiana is represented by the large star above the torch.
Capital	Indianapolis
Nickname	The Hoosier State

Motto	"The Crossroads of America"
Size (in area)	38th largest
Bird	cardinal
River	The Wabash River
Stone	limestone
Flower	peony
Tree	tulip tree
Industry	agriculture, including corn, dairy, chickens, hay, soybeans, and pork, and manufacturing, including auto parts, electronics, and steel

CIRCUS CLOWN MASK

For more than one hundred years, Peru, Indiana, has been thought of as the Circus Capital of the World.

What you will need

* pencil
* large paper plate
* scissors
* yarn or fake hair
* white glue
* poster paint
* paintbrush
* glitter pen
* hole punch
* paper reinforcements

In the 1870s there were many circuses. The big circuses used trains to get from town to town. Famous circus clowns and performers rode the trains that stopped in Peru, Indiana. Many circus folk settled down in Peru, Indiana, when their work with the circus was finished. Emmett Kelly, a very famous clown, lived in Peru.

What you will do

1. Draw eyes, a round circle for the nose, and a mouth, in pencil, on the back of a paper plate (See A).

A)

2. Cut out the eyes and mouth. Cut halfway around the circle for the nose (See B).

3. Glue the yarn or fake hair on the top of the head (See C). Let dry.

4. Paint around the eyeholes and mouth. Paint the nose red. Use a glitter pen to decorate the face (See D). Let dry.

5. Punch a hole near the edge of the mask on each side, below the eyes. Add paper reinforcements to the front and back of each hole.

6. Use the mask as a decoration. If you wish to wear it, cut two 12-inch pieces of yarn. Tie one piece through a paper-reinforced hole; do the same with the second piece of yarn. Ask an adult to tie the mask around your head.

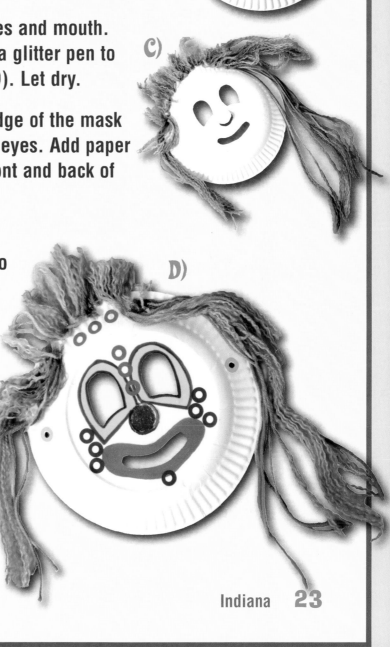

B)

C)

D)

VINTAGE RACE CAR

The Indianapolis Motor Speedway is a famous racetrack. The Speedway was built in 1909. It was first used as a place to test cars. The first race was held in 1911. At the Indianapolis Motor Speedway Hall of Fame, there are many vintage race cars.

What you will need

* scissors
* small cereal box or juice box
* hole punch
* pencil
* cardboard
* ruler
* soda straw
* poster paint
* paintbrush
* glitter pens
* white glue
* small yellow pom-poms
* markers

What you will do

1. Cut one long side out of a small cereal box or juice box. Punch a hole close to each end of the long, narrow sides of the box. Make sure the opposite holes line up. You should have four holes.

2. Draw a 1/4-inch circle on cardboard and cut it out. (See page 44 for the pattern.) Trace three more circles. Cut out the circles. Ask an adult to help you use the hole punch to make a hole in the center of each circle. Cut a straw in half.

3. Paint the car your favorite color. Let dry. Use glitter pens to add a racing number if you wish. Glue on yellow pom-poms for headlights. Add details with markers. Let dry.

4. Push one straw through two holes on one end of the cereal box. Add a circle to the each end of the straw. Repeat on the other end of the box with the other straw.

ILLINOIS

Origin of name	The name *Illinois* comes from the American Indian word *ilini*, which means "man" or "warrior."
Flag	The Illinois state flag shows the Great Seal of Illinois on a white background. The seal has an American bald eagle holding a banner with the state motto, "State Sovereignty, National Union" on it.
Capital	Springfield
Nickname	Land of Lincoln, The Prairie State

ILLINOIS

Motto	"State Sovereignty, National Union"
Size (in area)	25th largest
Animal	white-tailed deer
Bird	cardinal
Fish	bluegill
Flower	violet
Tree	white oak
Industry	farming, mining, manufacturing

RAG DOLL

From ancient times, most dolls were made of rags, wood, clay, or bone. Johnny Gruelle was an artist and a writer. He made a design for the first Raggedy Ann doll in 1915. Gruelle wrote a book called *Raggedy Ann Stories*. The Johnny Gruelle Raggedy Ann and Andy Museum is in Arcola, Illinois. Create your own rag doll.

What you will need

* pencil
* tracing paper
* poster board
* scissors
* felt
* yarn
* white glue
* two buttons
* large and small scrap pieces of felt in different colors
* cotton balls

What you will do

1. Trace the rag doll pattern onto poster board. (See page 46 for the pattern.) Cut it out. Trace the pattern onto felt. Trace it again to make two shapes. Cut out both shapes.

2. Cut pieces of yarn for hair. Glue them
to the doll's head on one of the felt
pieces. On the other shape, glue two
buttons onto the face for eyes. Draw a
small triangle on a small piece of
scrap felt for a nose. Cut it out, and
glue to the face. Draw a mouth on the
scrap felt. Cut it out, and glue to the doll's
face. Let dry.

3. Place the poster board pattern on a large
piece of scrap felt. Draw around the pattern
to make a shirt, dress, or pants that will fit
your doll. Cut out, and
glue to the doll. Let dry.

4. Glue the two parts of the
doll together. Leave the
head unglued. Let dry.
Stuff the doll with cotton
balls. Glue the head
closed. Let dry.

SAUK AND FOX NATION FLAG

Chief Black Hawk was born in Illinois in 1767. He was a leader of the Sauk Indians of northern Illinois. Chief Black Hawk believed that the land could not be bought or sold because it was given to the Indians by the Great Spirit. By 1828, the Sauk and Fox Indians were forced to leave their land.

What you will need

* ruler
* black marker
* 8 1/2-inch x 11-inch poster board
* red felt
* green felt
* scissors
* white glue
* one yard of white ribbon
* clear tape

Chief Black Hawk fought many battles trying to keep a homeland for his people. Make the green and red Sauk and Fox Nation flag.

What you will do

1. Draw a line from the middle of the short side to the middle of the opposite short side of the poster board with a marker, dividing the poster board into two equal size rectangles (See A).

2. Cut a piece of red felt the size of one rectangle. Cut a piece of

green felt the size of the other rectangle. Place the poster board so that the line in the center is horizontal. Glue the green felt on the top of the poster board. Glue the red felt on the bottom. Let dry.

A)

3. Cut one 8 1/2-inch piece of white ribbon. Make sure the green felt is at the top of the flag. Glue the white ribbon onto the left edge of the flag (See B). Let dry.

4. Cut a 12-inch piece of white ribbon. Tape the ends to the top corners on the back of the flag for hanging.

B)

WISCONSIN

Origin of name	**The name *Wisconsin* comes from the Chippewa Indian word meaning "grassy place."**
Flag	**The state flag of Wisconsin is dark blue. It has the name of the state printed in white over the state seal. Below the state seal is 1848, the year that Wisconsin joined the union. Above the state coat of arms is the state motto, "Forward," in a white scroll. The state animal, a badger, is below the scroll. A sailor and a miner are pictured on the left and right of the coat of arms.**
Capital	**Madison**

Nickname	The Badger State
Motto	"Forward"
Size (in area)	23rd largest
Animal	badger
Bird	robin
Fish	muskellunge
Flower	wood violet
Tree	sugar maple
Industry	agriculture, dairy, manufacturing

SCRAP SCULPTURE

The artist Dr. Evermore, also known as Tom Every, made sculptures near Baraboo, Wisconsin. He used pieces of scrap metal he found to make unusual objects. Dr. Evermore made a bird band with over forty scrap metal birds, a giant spider, and a vehicle with a canopy and a barbecue pit!

What you will need

NOTE: Ask an adult before you use any object!

Found objects such as:
* bottle caps
* twigs
* straws
* hairpins
* toothpicks
* craft foam scraps
* scissors
* white glue
* glitter pens
* markers

What you will do

1. Collect some found objects, such as bottle caps, twigs, straws, hairpins, and toothpicks.

2. Using small pieces of craft foam scraps, cut out some fun shapes. Glue the found objects and craft foam shapes together to form your own scrap sculpture. Let dry. Decorate parts of the sculpture with glitter pens and markers. Let dry.

3. Display your sculpture. What other sculptures can you create?

WHERE IS HOUDINI?

Harry Houdini was a famous magician who lived in Appleton, Wisconsin. Houdini performed his magic for many people from the 1890s through the 1920s. He could escape from police handcuffs and even escaped when he was tied up and hung upside down! The Houdini Historical Center in Appleton is an interesting place to learn more about Harry Houdini.

What you will need

* three 1/2-pint cream or juice cartons, washed and dried
* scissors
* poster paint
* paintbrush
* white glue
* rhinestones
* glitter pens
* self-hardening clay

What you will do

1. Cut the tops off three clean 1/2-pint cream or juice cartons.

2. Paint the cartons. Let dry. Glue rhinestones, and with the glitter pens, draw moons and stars on the cartons, trying to make all the cartons look the same. Let dry.

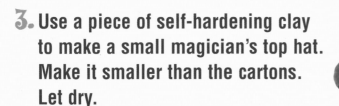

3. Use a piece of self-hardening clay to make a small magician's top hat. Make it smaller than the cartons. Let dry.

4. Paint the hat black, and let dry. Draw an H for Houdini on the hat with a glitter pen. Let dry.

5. Put the hat under one carton. Move all the cubes around quickly with your eyes closed. Where is Houdini— can you guess?

MINNESOTA

Origin of name	Minnesota's name comes from a Dakota Indian word that means "cloudy water" or "sky-tinted water."
Flag	The Minnesota state flag is blue, and has a gold border with a gold-fringed edge. Scenes from the Great Seal of the State of Minnesota are in a circle in the center. Since Minnesota is the nineteenth state to enter the Union, nineteen gold stars are around the center emblem. The year 1858 is printed in gold and stands for the year that Minnesota became a state. Red letters spelling *Minnesota* are underneath the emblem. A farmer and an American Indian are shown in the center of the circle, with the state flower, the showy lady's slipper, surrounding the scene. A red ribbon has *L'Etoile du Nord* printed on it in yellow letters, which means "Star of the North." The left side of the red ribbon has the year 1819 on it, representing the year Fort Snelling was built. On the right side is the date 1893, the year the flag was adopted.

Capital	Saint Paul
Nickname	The North Star State
Motto	*L'Etoile du Nord* (This is a Latin phrase which means, "The Star of the North.")
Size (in area)	12th largest
Bird	common loon
Fish	walleye
Flower	showy lady's slipper
Grain	wild rice
Tree	Norway pine
Industry	dairy, livestock, agriculture, mining, processed foods, electronics, computers

WILLIE WALLEYE PENCIL HOLDER

What you will need

* pencil
* poster board scrap
* scissors
* craft foam
* white glue
* markers
* glitter pen
* round oatmeal container
* construction paper
* clear tape

Fishing is popular in Minnesota, and the walleye is the state fish. There are large statues of this fish in different towns in the state. Baudette, Minnesota, has a forty-foot-long, two-ton, steel-and-concrete statue of a fish named Willie Walleye.

What you will do

1. Draw a fish shape on poster board scrap. (See page 45 for the pattern.) Cut out the shape. Trace around the shape on a piece of craft foam. Cut out the fish. Glue the foam fish onto the poster board. Let dry. Add details with markers and a glitter pen.

2. Cover the oatmeal container with construction paper. Cut the paper to fit the container, and wrap it around the container. Tape the edge. Glue the fish to the oatmeal container near the bottom. Make sure the opening of the container is at the top. Let dry.

3. Write "Willie the Walleye" on the oatmeal container with the glitter pen. Let dry. Decorate the rest of the oatmeal container as you like. Let dry. Place your pencils or crayons inside.

ICE CASTLE

In 1886, the first winter carnival was held in St. Paul, Minnesota. A large, beautiful castle made of ice was built. The ice blocks were carved from lakes in Minnesota. Ice castles continue to be an important part of the winter carnival.

What you will need

* two small juice boxes
* paintbrush
* white poster paint
* black marker
* shoe box
* white glue
* scissors
* silver and blue glitter

What you will do

1. Paint all but the bottom of the two juice boxes white. Let dry. Draw ice blocks on the boxes with a black marker. Let dry.

2. Turn the shoe box upside down. Glue the juice boxes, unpainted side down, near the short ends of the shoe box. Let dry.

3. Paint the shoe box white. Let dry. Draw a door with black marker, and cut it so it will open. Draw ice blocks with black marker. Decorate the ice castle with silver and blue glitter. Let dry.

PATTERNS

Use tracing paper to copy the patterns on these pages. Ask an adult to help you cut and trace the shapes.

Cherry Table Runner

At 100%

Vintage Race Car

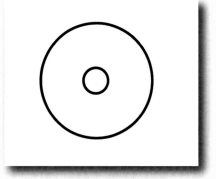

At 100%

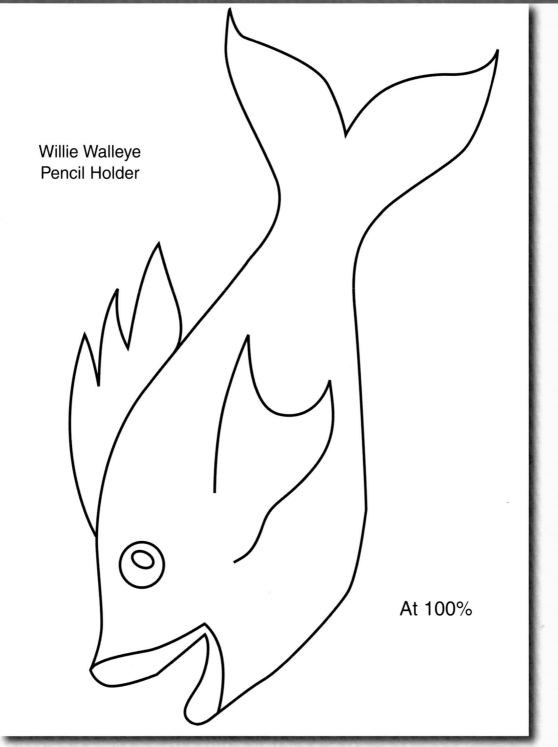

Willie Walleye
Pencil Holder

At 100%

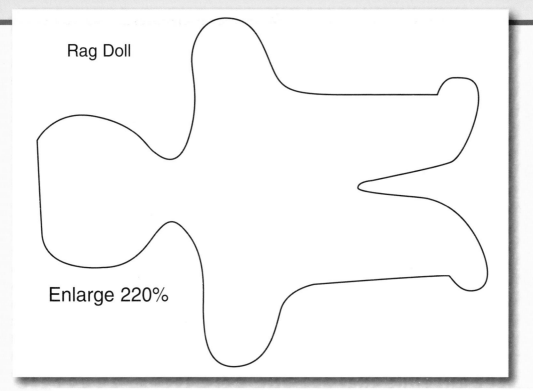

Rag Doll

Enlarge 220%

Hopewell Bird

At 100%

LEARN MORE

Books

Deady, Kathleen W. *Ohio*. Milwaukee, Wisc.: Gareth Stevens, 2006.

Derzipilski, Kathleen. *Indiana*. New York: Benchmark Books, 2007.

Haney, Johannah. *Michigan*. New York: Marshall Cavendish Benchmark, 2005.

Hasday, Judy L. *Minnesota*. New York: Children's Press, 2008.

Heinrichs, Ann. *Illinois*. Chanhassen, Minn.: Child's World, 2006.

Wargin, Kathy-Jo. *B is for Badger: A Wisconsin Alphabet*. Chelsea, Mich.: Sleeping Bear Press, 2004.

Internet Addresses

50states.com
<http://www.50states.com/>

U.S. States
<http://www.enchantedlearning.com/usa/states/>

INDEX